NAVIGATING YOUR NEW YORK CONTESTED DIVORCE CASE

David I. Bliven, Esq.

Jacobs & Whitehall
9600 Escarpment Blvd
Suite 745-282
Austin, TX 78749
www.jacobsandwhitehall.com

Ordering Information:

Quantity sales. Special discounts are available on quantity purchases by corporations, associations, and others. For details, contact the publisher at the address above.

Orders by U.S. trade bookstores and wholesalers. Please contact Jacobs & Whitehall: Tel: (888) 570-7338 or visit www.jacobsandwhitehall.com.

Printed in the United States of America

Published in 2023

ISBN: 978-1-954506-83-1

PREFACE

The overwhelming majority of divorce cases are resolved at the "uncontested" stage. Indeed, some of the latest statistics show that approximately 90% of divorce cases end at the uncontested stage[1].

"Uncontested" simply means the parties are able to resolve the case with an out-of-court settlement agreement - or if there are no children, property or any other issue which needs to be addressed in such an agreement, perhaps merely with "affidavits."

"Contested" means that the parties are unable to resolve the case at the uncontested phase - and therefore want a Judge to rule on the outstanding issues. In New York, either party has the right to contest the case at any point. Literally a party could

---

[1] https://www.forbes.com/advisor/legal/divorce/uncontested-divorce/#:~:text=At%20least%2090%25%20of%20all,to%20know%20about%20uncontested%20divorces.

theoretically contest the case from the minute it's filed – though this is very rarely done. The courts also have a rule requiring the parties to contest case if it's not resolved within 4 months after the Defendant is served with the summons[2].

Either party has an absolute right to contest the case – they can do so merely by filing a document called the "request for judicial intervention" ("RJI") – a long way of saying "I want to see the Judge." As such, if either party doesn't see the likelihood they will resolve the case within the 4-month window, then either party *should* file the RJI. That said, the court encourage the parties to make an earnest, good-faith effort to seek to resolve the case before getting a Judge involved. Settlements are sure things – what the Judge will do is not.

---

[2] If, during your review of this book, you get confused by the legal jargon, please consult this glossary on the court's website: https://nycourts.gov/Courthelp/goingtocourt/glossary.shtml#P.

Before contesting a divorce case, each party should strongly consider the time involved – a contested divorce case may last as long as 12-18 months or more (as opposed to several months to complete an uncontested divorce). Likewise, each party should consider the cost – if one has a good attorney representing him/her, it's likely the contested divorce will cost well into the ten's of thousands (in high income cases, it may run into the hundred's of thousands).

Moreover, each party should consider the stress a contested divorce cases will cost them – and their children. Unfortunately, contested divorces are avenues where parties often "air their dirty laundry" – many get quite nasty with insulting, degrading and embarrassing rhetoric heaved back and forth in an effort to score points with the Judge and/or get the other side to cave.

The purposes of this book is to guide you – the litigant or potential litigant – through the process of a contested divorce case. Some of the best preparation you can do for a contested divorce case occurs well before the case is even filed - planning budgets, gathering financial documents, and perhaps more importantly: gathering evidence to be used in the litigation.

One of the best cases I've been involved in which demonstrated this pre-litigation preparation involved a wife seeking a divorce form an abusive husband. She began tape-recording (both audio & video) his abusive threats and conduct towards her. She did this over the course of several months. When it came time for the divorce case, she had the audios transcribed and the attorney put them into a motion for supervised visitation and an order of protection. The Husband's ship was sunk before he even thought of preparing himself.

Another example stemmed from a case in which a wealthy husband wanted to get out of paying an enormous sum in maintenance (a/k/a alimony) & asset distribution. Thus, instead of filing for divorce right away, he convinced his wife to hold off on filing for divorce for several years. In those years, the kids all turned 21 (thus eliminating any child support obligation). He then started slowly winding down his business – each year it took in less & less money (at least one the books). When it came time for the divorce, it appeared (at least on paper) that he had relatively little income, the business wasn't doing well for many years & he didn't have all that much in assets left over to split. This is what I term the "slow bleed" of marital assets. The wife in that case was left on the defensive – trying to argue (in vein) that the divorce Judge should award her maintenance on income which no longer existed & award her a share of assets which had disappeared. Not a good position to find oneself in!

To protect against "getting the short end of the stick," litigants should consult a good divorce attorney as soon as one sees the marriage heading for an end. One should also review this book – along with my collection of other books, including "Navigating Your New York Divorce Case," "Navigating Your New York Family Court Case," Navigating Your New York Post-Divorce Case: Modifications and Enforcement," as well as the forthcoming book "Navigating Your New York Divorce Agreement Case."

And while this book is centered on divorce cases, if you have a contested custody, visitation or child support cases pending in New York Family Court, you will find this book helpful as well. Such cases deserve just as much preparation and planning as divorce cases do.

A final word: while my books hopefully provide a useful guide and will help you prepare & help you better assist your attorney, *do not try this alone*! "One who represents oneself has a fool for a client." Unless you're confident you have the time to read, absorb and comprehend thousands of pages of divorce statutes and treatises, the best advice I have is to retain a good attorney[3].

[3] Beyond Google, some of the more reputable websites to find a lawyer are: SuperLawyers, Findlaw, Legalmatch, and Avvo.

DISCLAIMER

This publication is intended to be used for educational purposes only. No legal advice is being given, and no attorney-client relationship is intended to be created by reading this material. The author assumes no liability for any errors or omissions or for how this book or its contents are used or interpreted, or for any consequences resulting directly or indirectly from the use of this book. For legal or any other advice, please consult an experienced attorney or the appropriate expert, who is aware of the specific facts of your case and is knowledgeable in the law in your jurisdiction.

The Law Offices of David Bliven

www.blivenlaw.net

White Plains Office
19 Court St.
Suite 206
White Plains, NY 10601
(914) 468-0968

Bronx Office
3190 Riverdale Avenue
Suite 1
Bronx, NY 10463
(718) 725-9600

TABLE OF CONTENTS

CHAPTER 1

HEADING FOR A CONTESTED DIVORCE?

The vast majority of divorces ultimately end as **uncontested divorces**, meaning they ultimately settle outside of Court and do not require litigation.

A divorce case becomes **contested** when either:

a. The parties attempt to negotiate a resolution outside of a courtroom and are unsuccessful in doing so; or,

b. The parties know right from the outset that they are not going to be able to negotiate a resolution outside of a courtroom.

There are a number of different scenarios in which a divorcing couple might know from the outset that they won't be able to negotiate successfully outside of a courtroom. This commonly happens in cases involving domestic violence, or otherwise deeply troubled relationships in which communication has completely broken down.

Negotiation might also be a non-starter in cases where there are sharply contested custody issues. These issues are often difficult to negotiate outside of a courtroom - in large part because the stakes and the emotions involved are so high that parties are less likely to be able to reach a compromise.

For instance, let's say Parent A leaves the family home with the children and wants full custody, and Parent B is contesting the issue of custody and wants the child to be returned. In a case like that, there is often no "middle ground" the parties can agree upon, and mediation outside of litigation is typically fruitless.

If both parties know right off the bat that mediation or negotiation won't work, then there's usually no point in continuing to pursue it. Instead, you may as well contest the case from the outset. This means filing a document called a **"Request for Judicial Intervention ("RJI").**[4]"

A Request for Judicial Intervention is the form to ask the Court to assign a Judge to the case. Usually, the Court will respond to a Request for Judicial Intervention by setting up a **preliminary conference**[5], which is the first meeting with a Judge and/or their Court Attorney, and/or a Referee. Whether you meet with a Judge, their Court Attorney, a Referee, or all three depends on the Court in question.

It is important to note that a contested case can become an uncontested case at any time. At any step of

---

4 https://www.nycourts.gov/legacypdfs/forms/rji/UCS-840.pdf

5 Some court will require you to separately submit the "Request for Preliminary Conference form" - https://www.nycourts.gov/legacyPDFs/courts/6jd/forms/SRForms/req_prelimconf.pdf

the way, the parties can opt to negotiate and/or go into mediation outside of a courtroom – and thereby seek to settle the case. Indeed, roughly 95-98% of all divorce cases settle at some point before a trial ruling—including many cases which were fiercely contested when they began.

The point being, even if you have a contested divorce case, you can still settle – and even after a trial has actually commenced. Judges and court attorneys encourage settlement at every step of the way, as that is considered the desired outcome of divorce cases.

The other option to proceed on a contested case is to file an **Order to Show Cause**. This is usually done in case of emergencies, or to address any urgent or emergency issues. For instance, parties might file:

- **A request for an interim Order of Protection,** sometimes referred to as a "restraining order", which may compel the other party to keep a certain distance from the filing party, and to refrain from contacting them.

- **A request for an interim Order of Custody,** in which one party seeks full or partial custody of the children, either indefinitely or for the duration of the divorce process
- **A request for an Order of Exclusive Occupancy,** in which one party seeks to remove the other party from a shared residence.

In a nutshell, it is each party's right to contest a divorce at any time. What "contested divorce" means is that the parties really don't foresee being able to settle the case through mere negotiation or mediation outside of a courtroom, and need the intervention of a Judge and potentially a trial.

What are the Most Common Reasons That Couples Find Themselves in a Contested Divorce Situation?

In my experience, the most common reasons that couples find themselves in contested divorce situations are:

a. **Sharply contested custody or visitation issues**

b. Very steep requests for asset distribution and/or spousal maintenance (otherwise known as "alimony")

In either of these cases, the dispute would have to be so severe that there is no middle ground and negotiation is not possible.

For example, let's say the parties are trying to negotiate a resolution on custody issues. Often, attorneys will try to recommend that their clients try to find a compromise, and possibly settle for some kind of joint or shared custody. However, in cases where both parents absolutely insist that they want primary physical custody, the idea of joint or shared custody isn't really applicable. If both parties are absolutely set on fighting for full physical custody and refuse to accept anything less under any circumstances, further negotiation is going to be fruitless.

The same concept applies to contested issues around visitation. For instance, let's say that Parent A insists that Parent B shouldn't have overnight visits, or should only have supervised visits, and Parent B refuses to accept those terms. There may be good reasons for Parent A's insistence: Parent B could have drug or alcohol issues, or perhaps mental health issues. On the other hand, there may be good reasons for Parent B's insistence: Parent A could be acting out of spite or vindictiveness, or perhaps fabricating reasons to withhold the child from Parent B. In a case like this, you are unlikely to get either parent to budge on their position, and further attempts at negotiation or mediation in search of a "compromise" are consequently unlikely to work.

You could also have a parent claim s/he wants shared custody, but they want it to be organized in a particular way the other parent does not agree with. In such a case, the attorneys for both sides will do their jobs and try negotiating a solution which works for everyone, usually by proposing various ways to settle the issue.

For example, let's say two parties, Parent A and Parent B, come in with this sort of case. Parent A is insisting that out of every two weeks (14 nights), they should have the children for 9 nights, and the other parent should only get the children for 5 nights. Parent B is insisting on a strict 7-night/7-night even split.

Alternatives include proposing a compromise of perhaps an 8-night/6-night split or alternating 9-night/5-night splits every two weeks - if the issue has to do with weekday versus weekend scheduling.

It's worth mentioning that sometimes getting a Judge assigned to a contested case is a good thing. In some cases, people really don't want to hear from their attorneys what the best course of action is, and it can really pay to hear basically the same information from a Judge. Judges can listen to the details of the case as presented in that first meeting, and can reason candidly with one or both parties about the likely outcome if they move forward with a hearing. They can do so with an air of authority that some people find more compelling than the advice of his/her own attorney.

Of course, this is not a "pre-judgement" - Judges will qualify that they're not telling the parties what they *will* decide once all of the evidence and testimonies are laid out before them at a full trial. However, they can say what they have heard about the situation up to that point does not support one or both parties' case for the particular issue they're disputing.

Sometimes, if parties hear this sort of honest estimation from a Judge, they become much more likely to settle or to consider re-entering negotiations. Other times, talking to a Judge does not have this effect. Two different people can hear the same thing from a Judge and have wildly different reactions: one can decide that a settlement is a better idea, and another might double down on their position and insist on moving forward with a hearing. In the case of the former, the next step is to re-enter negotiations or broker a settlement if the parties are ready. In the case of the latter, the next step is to continue down the road to a trial.

Chapter 2

Preparing For A Contested Divorce

Though it may be more difficult to prepare for a contested divorce if you're dealing with an uncooperative spouse, it is possible to do so. Your preparation should focus on the areas where you think the other party is most likely to raise opposition or refuse to cooperate.

For instance, let's say you are concerned the other party isn't going to give you a separate property credit for putting premarital funds into your shared marital residence. In that case, you can prepare by gathering as much evidence of the pre-marital contribution as possible.

There are many different ways of gathering this sort of information. Sometimes you have to go back to the real estate attorney who represented you when you were buying the house to get the closing statement. You may have to go to your bank to get copies of checks which were cut, or copies of old bank statements that attest to your premarital funds. These pieces of evidence might be in the bank's archives, which means you may have to pay a fee and wait - sometimes for several months - for the bank to give you a copy. It is advisable to start gathering this sort of evidence as soon as possible if you foresee the other party is not going to settle on a given issue.

If the other party is going to contest custody issues, there are also different ways you can prepare. For one, you can start lining up testimonial statements from unbiased people who are involved with your child or children, such as teachers, guidance counselors, principals, doctors, sports coaches, youth group leaders, and people who head up your children's extracurricular activities. These testimonial statements should speak to your involvement with the children and/or the relative lack of involvement of their other parent. They can be simple statements of fact, involving things like which parent brings the children to school and which parent picks them up.

If your children's school or extracurricular activity center keeps sign-in lists, you should also get copies of those records. You should be able to contact the school administration and see if you can get copies in advance. Sometimes, schools have policies not to release those sorts of records without a subpoena. In that case, simply report the information back to your attorney, and s/he can prepare a subpoena for the records if they are necessary.

The key here is to request all potentially relevant documentation from the various entities where they are kept. If people are willing to simply give you copies of various documents, it's a lot faster and easier than having your attorney prepare and execute a subpoena.

Especially if you're still residing with the other parent, begin tape-recording (or videotaping) negative interactions with him/her (or between him/her & the child). In one case, a Mother tape-recorded the Father making severe threats of harm towards her during arguments – which served her well in winning custody.

You can also tape-record the other parent admitting to things. For example: if the Father has an alcohol issue but is threatening to contest custody, the Mother can turn-on the voice memo app on her phone, stick it in her pocket, and then strike-up a conversation with the Father by saying "Look, I'd like to work-out custody with you, but I'm concerned that if you have custody of our daughter, your drinking issues may impact your ability to take care of her. I might be more amenable to shared custody if you would get help for your issue." Then see what he says – if he acknowledges (even implicitly or by silence) having an alcohol issue, now you have corroborating evidence.

You can also take pictures to corroborate drug/alcohol issues. In another case I handled the mother took pictures of the trash can filled with empty liquor bottles each week. Keep a paper-trail with your spouse – for example, e-mails or texts confirming your versions of events or communications relevant to the custody issues.

Another thing to consider is possibly hiring a private investigator, a forensic accountant, a forensic psychologist, or any other type of expert investigator or witness. Depending on the issues being contested in your case and what evidence an expert is likely to uncover, it may be a good idea to hire a specific type of expert for investigative/evidence-gathering and testimonial purposes.

Notably, not all cases call for the use of one of these experts. This is especially true if your finances are limited—as is often the case when people are going through a divorce—since they tend to be very costly. You should discuss the relative merits of hiring a particular expert with your attorney. In many cases, evidence that an expert might uncover can be found just as easily through the normal course of discovery, which is a pre-trial stage every contested divorce goes through.

For example, let's say you are getting divorced, and you receive a "net worth statement" from your ex which does not report a house in another state which you know about and believe they own. In this case, some people might assume you need to hire a private investigator or forensic accountant - but there are other things you can try first.

One option would be to conduct an online property search. For example, in the NYC area, one can do a search by a person's name & find all the property associated with him/her[6].

---

[6] https://a836-acris.nyc.gov/CP/

Another option would be to send out a **Demand for Interrogatories**[7]. This is essentially a series of questions the other party will have to answer under oath. You can pose specific questions to address or try to weed out specific issues.

In this case, one potential question you could pose is, "Do you own any other property or have any other property anywhere in the world other than those you have listed on your net worth statement?" If they answer yes, then they will have to disclose the house as an asset, and there is no need to hire a private investigator or forensic accountant. If they say no, on the other hand, then they are obviously committed to hiding the house as an asset, and you will most likely need expert investigators to track down the

---

[7] An example of an interrogatory demand, albeit in the custody context (though it's similar to those used on financial issues as well), can be found here: https://www.google.com/url?client=internal-element-cse&cx=007303269921793870550:_q2pkzn2t1i&q=https://www.nycourts.gov/courts/ad4/AFC/Forms/Custody/Interrogatories.doc&sa=U&ved=2ahUKEwj4pNKO_tz_AhVmGFkFHeHoDz0QFnoECAUQAQ&usg=AOvVaw3PHgrgAxEl9YZJnOmN8sj3

evidentiary proof that the house exists and they own it (for instance, the deed or title).

How Long Does a Contested Divorce Usually Take to Resolve?

Typically, from start to finish, contested divorce cases usually take 1-2 years to resolve (at least in the greater NYC area). They can be shorter or longer than that - depending on the case & the court. I have had some really bad and very contentious cases that lasted for many years.

In fact, one case I was involved in wound up lasting 8 years. There were particular circumstances behind the case as to why it lasted that long. One was that my client was extremely litigious. I was his 6th attorney, and by the time I signed on to the case, my predecessors had already taken it up to the appellate division twice and received decisions reversing the trial court both times, resulting in new trials.

Of course, that is an extreme example. More often than not, contested divorce cases will not last longer than two years, and a good deal of them will not last much longer than one year.

One of the main reasons contested divorce cases take as long as they do is because the process has a number of stages, each of which have to be placed on the Court's schedule. In addition, each of these stages can be adjourned, which is when a hearing phase is stopped to provide time for one or both parties to complete a task or meet a requirement. When an adjournment happens, a new date must be scheduled to continue that part of the trial or pre-trial. These dates are often spaced out rather distantly from one another - especially in the greater New York City area.

For example, the normal course of a contested divorce case involves three separate conferences—a Preliminary Conference, a Compliance Conference, and a Pre-Trial Conference—all before the trial even begins. The date for the trial isn't even set until the Pre-Trial Conference. Any one of those conferences can be adjourned, sometimes more than once, with an average of 2-3 months between adjournment and the rescheduled date. On average, in a given contested divorce case, there will be 3-5 pre-trial court appearances before one even hits the trial.

When it comes to the trial itself, proceedings also happen over the course of several Court dates. Typically, contested divorce trials take 3 to 5 dates to complete - but it all depends on the case in question and which specific issues are being contested (as well as how many hours the Judge gives the case on any particular day). If both custody/visitation issues and financial issues (like spousal support, child support, and division of assets) are being contested, you may actually have somewhere between 5-10 trial dates. On the other hand, if there is only one limited issue being tried, it's possible the trial could be completed in around 1-2 days.

CHAPTER 3

DOMESTIC VIOLENCE ACCUSATIONS & CUSTODY DISPUTES: PRELIMINARY THOUGHTS

Domestic violence accusations can affect a contested divorce in several different ways.

The first pertains to decisions about any children shared by the divorcing couple. Domestic violence is a specific statutory factor **that can affect custody and visitation decisions.**

Beyond custody and visitation matters, domestic violence can also affect things like **spousal maintenance and asset distribution.** The argument often made in that context is the domestic violence affected or inhibited the survivor's ability to earn income or go to school. A survivor could argue the domestic violence affected them so severely it impeded their ability to apply themselves and reach their full potential. In those cases, the Courts can take domestic violence into consideration as a factor in their Decisions.

One may wish to consider having a pre-trial report prepared by one's therapist or by a certified mental health professional[8] who can attest whether the domestic violence occurred and how it affected the party in the ways s/he claims it did.

This has to do with the way things are proven in a legal context. The client simply stating their "opinion" that it happened and it affected them in a certain way is usually inadmissible in terms of linking

---

[8] https://www.jurispro.com/category/spousal-abuse-s-505

their inability to work/go to school with the other party's acts of domestic violence.

In order for domestic violence to affect something like spousal maintenance or division of assets, we have to prove two elements:

1. That the other party perpetuated domestic violence against the victim and that it made an impact on them psychologically/emotionally (or even physically); AND,
2. That the impact made by the other party's domestic violence impacted the victim's ability to work, go to school, and/or develop themselves professionally.

If your aim is to have a domestic violence claim affect spousal maintenance/the division of assets, you should have corroboration from a mental health professional on-hand. If all you have is the survivor's self-reported experience (without corroboration), you are unlikely to be successful in your argument.

In Contested Divorce Cases Where There are Custody Disputes, What Happens to the Children During the Divorce Process?

In contested divorce cases where custody is being disputed, **the Judge will usually look to maintain the status quo for the children.** Matters like custody are decided primarily based on the best interest of the children, and maintaining the "status quo" (i.e., a situation as close as possible to the way things were before the divorce) is often considered to be in the best interest of the children.

If there's already an informally established schedule for the children, the access schedule and custody status will usually be modeled after that schedule for the duration of the divorce proceedings. In contested divorces involving contested custody, the Court does try to move the case toward a relatively quick custody trial, in which they can make an informed determination about what the access schedule should be on a permanent or semi-permanent basis.

Sometimes, though, the parties are not able to agree, and the Court is not able to hear the divorce case quickly enough. In those instances, either party can ask the Court to set an **interim custody arrangement or visitation schedule,** which will usually stand for the duration of the divorce proceedings.

For example, let's say Party A and Party B have one child. They decide to physically separate, and the child remains in the family home with Party A. Party A says she is fine with Party B seeing the child once a week. Party B says that once a week is not acceptable, and instead says he wants custody of the child every other weekend, from Friday afternoon to Monday morning.

If Party A and Party B are not able to negotiate toward some kind of compromise or middle ground, then Party B—generally speaking—would be entitled to make an Application to a Judge (usually through an Order to Show Cause), asking that the Judge set an **interim visitation schedule** as enforced by the Court.

This would involve Party B providing an affidavit as to why he feels it is right and proper for the

Court to grant him the relief (i.e., why he feels the Court should rule in favor of his proposed visitation schedule). Then, Party A would be able to voice her objections to the arguments made by Party B and make her own arguments.

In some cases, this process will take the form of a **"mini-hearing",** in which the Court will hear from each party about their reasoning and will be able to subject both parties to cross-examination without having to conduct a full **interim hearing**. These "mini hearings" are sometimes used instead of full interim hearings because conducting full interim hearings for custody can be an incredibly involved process. They can take quite a long time, which ultimately may wind up defeating the purpose of an "interim resolution," and can be disruptive to the life of the child.

The Judge knows if custody is ultimately going to be contested during the divorce proceedings, then that process will just have to be repeated in the full trial. What's more, during the full trial, both sides will actually have the ability to present their arguments fully. Each side will have their full repertoire of evidence, usually including home study reports, forensic psychological reports and other evidence which was not included in the interim hearing.

As such, if there already is an informal arrangement in place which more or less matches the pre-separation status quo for the child, Judges are sometimes cautious about establishing a different custody or visitation arrangement before the full arguments get made again during the divorce proceedings.

Nevertheless, if there are domestic violence issues involved, then the Court may need to order a CPS investigation – and/or a forensic mental health evaluation to determine what impact, if any, the domestic violence has on parenting capacity. In severe and/or repeated instances of domestic violence, the Judge may make the perpetrator's access to the children supervised until the pre-trial investigations take place.

CHAPTER 4

TIMELINE FOR A CONTESTED DIVORCE

Contested Divorce Timeline

After getting a summons for divorce, you generally have 20 days to respond. One usually hires an attorney to formally respond to the summons within that time.

If you get served a summons with notice, you just have to enter a *Notice of Appearance*, usually done by an attorney. If you get served with a summons and complaint, you have to file an answer to the complaint[9].

Merely filing an answer—even if this includes a counterclaim—does *not* mean the case is contested. A contested divorce case happens when a *request for judicial intervention* (RJI) is filed—meaning one wants a Judge formally assigned to the case.

Once an RJI is filed, the court commonly schedules a preliminary conference with the Judge or Referee. This date is often assigned within a few days to a week after you file the RJI. The actual court date will then usually be four to eight weeks into the future.

At the conference, the Court largely reviews the preliminary conference order - the form may be found here: *preliminary conference order*. You'd benefit from

---

[9] If you're going to handle that on your own, then sample forms for an Answer, Notice of Appearance & Affidavit of Service can be found here: https://www.nycourts.gov/LegacyPDFS/courts/12jd/bronx/civil/pdfs/How-to-Respond-to-a-Summons-and-Complaint-in-a-Divorce-case.pdf.

checking out the form before this conference – and to review the form with your lawyer - to prepare for the issues being discussed. Generally, the order addresses the discovery schedule as well as what issues are contested.

Additionally, prior to the preliminary conference, you're required to complete & submit a sworn net worth statement (to the degree you haven't done so already). The form may be found here: https://www.nycourts.gov/LegacyPDFS/forms/matrimonial/Net%20Worth%20Statement%20Form%20(Gender%20Neutral)%20rev.%20June%202016%20Eff.%208.1.16.pdf.

You should also discuss with your attorney whether you have grounds to submit an application for interim orders – such as interim orders of protection, for maintenance (a/k/a "alimony"), child support, or custody/visitation. The form for an order to show cause may be found here: https://www.nycourts.gov/LegacyPDFS/forms/matrimonial/PS-Temporary-Relief-OSC.pdf

During the preliminary conference, the Referee and/or Judge may have settlement suggestions for the parties if they're just a bit apart on the contested matters. If things cannot be resolved at that time, the next court date is for a compliance conference. At this meeting, the parties discuss with the court where they're at with *disclosure*—the exchanging of documents and information.

At the preliminary conference, the Court will also discuss submission of mandatory financial disclosure, including the net worth statement as well as the documents outlined below. The Court will strive to simplify and limit the issues which will be presented at trial - if the case does not settle beforehand (any issues left unresolved may be presented to the Judge at trial). The Court will also establish deadlines for the exchange of financial documentation, any necessary appraisals and/or experts, and depositions (if needed). If custody is an issue, the Court may appoint an Attorney to represent the Child(ren). You should thus be prepared to discuss interim arrangements for custody and parental access - you can get a head start by reviewing the court's proposed parenting plan order.

Usually, the deadline for disclosure is set up in the preliminary conference. For a wide variety of reasons, everything is not always done by the compliance conference. Sometimes people exchange some documents, but they don't exchange everything needed for litigation.

One should be aware that any issues as to grounds, custody, or finances which are not raised at the conference may be precluded from being subsequently raised. At the completion of the conference, the Court will ask all parties to sign-off on the preliminary conference order – your signature will acknowledge you understand all the information contained in the order and will follow its dictates.

Between the compliance conference and the pre-trial (or "trial-ready") conference, deposition and the completion of paper disclosure occur. The pre-trial conference is your final conference before the court sets to resolve the remaining disputes. The court will expect all disclosure issues to be resolved by the pre-trial conference, as well as references to attempts to resolve them. Most Judges and Referees will not accept excuses from attorneys or parties who don't do much to resolve disclosure issues. Those discussions should be had amongst counsel in an earnest attempt to resolve them before going into that final conference.

During the course of the contested divorce proceeding, each party is entitled to an exploration of the extent of marital property, the extent of separate property, to discover hidden assets and waste, and to develop information which may be relevant to the determination of the financial issues.

Each side is required by law to produce certain financial disclosure with regard to the equitable distribution issue. Should you fail to produce necessary financial disclosure, the court may assess sanctions against you, which may include precluding you from presenting proof of your income and finances. The list of this "**mandatory disclosure**" is as follows:

i. all paycheck stubs for the current calendar year and the last paycheck stub for the immediately preceding calendar year;

ii. all filed state and federal income tax returns for the previous three years including both personal returns and returns filed on behalf of any partnership or closely held corporation of which the party is a partner or shareholder;

iii. all W-2 wage and tax statements, 1099 forms, and K-1 forms for any year in the past three years in which the party did not file state and federal income tax returns;

iv. all statements of accounts received during the past three years from each financial institution in which the party has maintained an account in which cash or securities are held;

v. the statements immediately preceding and following the date of commencement of the matrimonial action pertaining to: (A) any policy of life insurance having a cash or dividend surrender value; and (B) any deferred compensation plan of any type or nature in which the party has an interest including, but not limited to Individual Retirement Accounts, pensions, profit-sharing plans, Keogh plans, 401K plans and other retirement plans.

At a "pretrial conference" date, the parties will have to submit - among other things - a proposed statement of disposition, updated net worth statements, and in some courts (including Westchester), both sides have to submit a "trial notebook." A trial notebook essentially consists of pre-tabbed exhibits that each party intends to put into evidence - along with witness lists[10].

If contested matters cannot be fully resolved at the pre-trial conference, the court sets the matter down for trial. They discuss with the attorneys how many days of trial to expect - depending on what is being contested. Typical trials take place over three to five dates. If both custody and financial disputes are involved, trials often last six to ten dates.

---

[10] Individual Judges may require additional contents of the "trial notebook" & thus one should consult the Judge's part Rules to verify what's due & when it's due.

CHAPTER 5

CONTESTED DIVORCE DISCOVERY IN NEW YORK

Discovery Process

Discovery in a contested divorce is the process of disclosing information, so you don't get to a trial with the other side whipping out evidence you've never seen before. In New York, this exchange can happen even before the preliminary conference. Parties may exchange supporting documents, like net worth statements, before the conference gets underway. Sometimes, this transfer of information even kicks off settlement negotiations.

Usually, the net worth statement is preliminary to settlement negotiations unless you are confident you know what the other side has. Perhaps you have filled out joint tax returns and know what assets the other side has. We need this statement for negotiations or a signed written waiver to move forward without it.

Other times discovery occurs before the preliminary conference to aid in settlement negotiations. Suppose either side wants to clarify specific issues, such as premarital credits, retirement accounts established before the marriage, or money spent in questionable ways. In that case, this information is often shared early on.

For instance, you request a premarital credit. You took money earned before the marriage to put towards the down payment of a house. Often, you need to get documentation to show both ends of the transaction. One needs to prove where the money came from and that the same money was put down at the closing. These special exchanges of information can happen early in the process.

According to the preliminary conference order, mandatory disclosure is three years' worth of financial statements must be produced by both sides from all accounts:

- Tax Returns (& W-2's/1099's)
- Bank accounts (Checking & Savings)
- Credit card/debt
- Investments
- Retirement accounts (pensions, IRS's, 401k's, annuities, deferred comp, etc.)

If you do not have paper copies of your financial statements, it is suggested that you access your provider's website and download the statements from there. If you do not have copies of your tax returns and cannot retrieve them from your tax preparer, then you should obtain the tax transcripts by accessing the IRS website (http://www.irs.gov/Individuals/Get-Transcript).

Parties often ask for more documentation than just the mandatory disclosure. This request is captured in the *demand for discovery and inspection.* Each side comes up with a list of documents they want produced by the other side. Often, there are about 20 to 30 categories of documents exchanged. If either side thinks the other is abusing that—asking for too much or irrelevant documentation—they have 20 days to object. If they miss the 20-day deadline, they generally have to answer it whether they like it or not.

Typical "discovery" demands include:

Demands for Discovery & Inspection. This is usually a vastly expanded list (beyond the "mandatory disclosure" list) of financial documents one must generally provide. Examples of other documents which are demanded are:

a. Business Expense records
b. Employment Contracts
c. Records of Employment-Related Fringe Benefits

d. Real Estate Documents, such as deeds & mortgage records.
e. Records of Rental Income
f. Documents Regarding Personal Property (such as receipts of large purchases)
g. Insurance Policies & Statements
h. Safe Deposit Box Documents
i. Documents Pertaining To Gifts Or Gambling Winnings
j. Estate Documents, Such As Copies Of Wills
k. Personal Financial Statements, Such As Applications For Credit Or Loans
l. Trust Documents
m. Documents Pertaining To Business Interests, Such As Corporate Returns & Records.
n. Vehicle Documents, Such As Titles & Registrations.
o. Separate Property & Claimed Credits Documents
p. Bankruptcy & Lien Records

Interrogatories. A list of up to 25 questions you must answer under oath.

Expert witness disclosure. A list of witnesses the other will produce at trial.

Audio, video, or pictorial evidence. Any evidence of this type that's going to be introduced at trial.

Statements. The oral or written statements of the other party so that there are no surprises at trial.

In a contested divorce case, these typical demands for disclosure are made after the preliminary conference. If one has an objection to providing any of this disclosure, s/he must register the particularized objection within 20 days of getting served with the demand – otherwise the Court may rule s/he effectively waived the right to object.

One of the aims of the disclosure is obtaining as much evidence the other side plans to produce as possible, apart from disclosure on custody and visitation issues[11]. There are some exceptions to

---

[11] Upstate NY courts tend to allow some pre-trial disclosure on custody/visitation issues – downstate courts usually do not.

discuss with your attorney around the appropriateness of asking for disclosure related to child-related issues.

There are statutory factors on asset distribution, child support maintenance, etc., that allow you to ask the other side if they have any physical or mental health issues. Sometimes issues are intertwined between custody, visitation, and financial issues – such as health (physical & mental) and domestic violence (now a statutory factor on both maintenance & asset distribution). In obtaining information on finances, you can ask if the other side has any limitations in working or accrual of assets. You can also ask if another side has a drug issue through the financial disclosure. You have a right to know where they're spending that money. It's an arguable marital waste issue if they spend marital money on drugs.

In contested cases, people often do depositions of both parties, and sometimes third parties. Depositions are where the parties are grilled under oath in the opposing attorney's conference room (with a reporter present). Some of the advantages in doing them are that they serve to lock in a party's testimony (so the attorney isn't questioning a witness for the first time at trial) and to learn information one cannot glean from financial documents themselves. Oftentimes depositions are held off until the very end of the case, simply because they are extremely expensive to do - in order to do a deposition, one is looking at a $5,000+ cost. If the case still can't settle, the deposition dates are usually scheduled at the compliance conference (though some courts require that presumptive dates be scheduled at the preliminary conference). If the case still can't settle at the final court date (called a "pre-trial conference"), all the discovery has been exchanged and all the forensic reports are in, then the Judge will schedule a trial.

Third-Party Testimony

Third parties with knowledge of your marriage can be questioned at a deposition in a contested divorce. If you don't have a really good reason for asking questions of the third party (particularly re-trial) - don't bother. Get the information from another source. There are also ways of subpoenaing documents. You don't necessarily have to ask questions of the third party - you can just ask them to produce certain documents.

To have them answer questions at a deposition, you would serve a deposition notice on that third party, along with a third-party subpoena and witness fee. Unless you anticipate they will be hostile or evade being served, you want to coordinate with the other party as best as possible to ensure they are available to appear. You will also be responsible for reimbursing them for any cost associated with travel for the deposition unless they appear virtually. In these post-pandemic days, virtual depositions are commonplace.

Accountants can be included in deposition questioning. You may want to subpoena accountants even after reviewing the documentation they have prepared to see what they discussed with this person. Generally, there's no privilege between an accountant and a party. What they discuss and the information provided may be relevant in your case. For example, if someone owns their own business and you suspect they are hiding money, you will want to ask the accountant specific questions such as: *What did you use to put down all these business expenses on their Schedule C? Did you see receipts or invoices?*

If the accountant explains the figures came directly from the party themselves, the party cannot later blame the accountant when you go to trial. They will be stuck with those figures, and they're going to have to justify them.

You should discuss with your attorney whether to send out subpoenas for documents along the way – as well as whether to retain experts such as a private investigator, forensic accountant or forensic psychologist (the latter particularly on contested custody cases). Private investigators and/or forensic accountants utilize many more tools to discover hidden income/assets - and do so often more cheaply and more effectively than an attorney would otherwise be able to do. If you are contending there are hidden income, assets, and/or property, then one should strongly consider hiring one if not both of these experts.

CHAPTER 6

NEW YORK CONTESTED DIVORCE SETTLEMENTS V. TRIALS

Settling Your Divorce

About 95 to 98% of contested divorce cases settle at some point. It's extremely rare that a case goes through trial completion with a trial decision. From the preliminary conference filing, right up until a trial begins, settlement is a possibility at any point along the road.

I'm completing a trial now where at almost every trial date, the Judge or the Court Attorney asks, "Okay, where are we at in terms of settlement?" The courts will always encourage settlement because it takes so much time and expense for a trial. It also takes a lot of time for the court & the attorneys to review the transcripts - and for the Judge to draft a decision. The Judges and Court Attorneys only have so much time to give to a particular case.

One should still prepare one's case as if it will go to trial – but this isn't a hard-and-fast rule. Just because a request for a preliminary conference is filed does not mean you can't anticipate a settlement. Often, when a preliminary conference request is filed, the attorneys and the parties are still actively negotiating a settlement.

When we get to the preliminary conference and tell the Referee or Judge those negotiations are ongoing, we'll request an extended disclosure schedule. We thus try to push the dates for completion of disclosure as far as they're willing to go to give the case some breathing room.

If the attorneys are not able to resolve the case themselves, often a four-way settlement conference or mediation is encouraged. With a 4-way conference, the parties and their attorneys sit down in a conference room for an open and frank discussion to resolve the remaining contested issues.

When To Go To Trial

It's worth going to trial for contested divorce support or custody matters if the parties' positions are totally opposed, and there's no middle ground. For example, Dad wants to have overnight visitation, and Mom opposes it. If there's no way to resolve that issue, you really have to take the case to trial.

Sometimes we can negotiate a kind of graduated schedule. If Mom's main concern is Dad isn't used to taking care of the child on his own, we try to resolve the case with a gradual schedule instead of going to trial. Perhaps at the three-month mark, Dad progresses to one overnight. At the six-month mark, two overnights every other week. If there are no issues at one year, then Dad progresses to a stage where he has Friday after school till Monday morning or something along those lines.

There are a variety of ways to settle the case. However, if you reach a point where we've explored every possible avenue of resolving the issues, and they just can't be settled, you have to take the case to trial.

We sometimes do a cost-benefit analysis to see if it is financially worth it to go to trial with financial issues. For example, a wife wants alimony (a/k/a maintenance) and asserts she is *presumptively entitled to alimony,* but the husband is unwilling to give her anything. We discuss every settlement variation, but the husband is not willing to give her anything in the ballpark of what she's asking for. The wife may see it as financially worth her while to take the case to trial because the odds are in her favor. She may spend $30 to $50 thousand at trial but will likely get $100 to $200 thousand in alimony. At that point, it's fiscally worth it to take the issue to trial.

On the other hand, let's say the wife's position is she's entitled to $100,000 in maintenance paid-out over several years (e.g., $1,500 monthly for roughly 5-6 years). And let's say Husband's position is he'd rather pay nothing in maintenance. Perhaps the case can be settled by reaching a middle ground – for instance, the Husband pays a $40,000 lump sum, the discounted amount based on the Husband paying everything up-front, rather than over the course of several years. When we identify wife needs money sooner rather than later, in such instances it may be worth it for her to accept less money as a compromise for getting it all up-front.

How Are Negotiations Handled in Contested Divorce Cases?

Contested divorces happen both in court and out of court, and the Judge (or his/her court attorney or a Referee) usually plays a role in negotiations. At the very least, the Judge will often get involved to gauge how far apart the parties are in settlement discussions. Sometimes there's a "Settlement Part," and the Judges will send the case out to a Referee to attempt to negotiate a settlement.

The Judges, Referees, and court attorneys are all there to make settlement suggestions. So, if they hear what both parties say, then based on their humble experience and as a neutral voice in the mix, they can sometimes think of alternatives which the parties' attorneys have not.

Suppose the husband is making a particular settlement position on a given issue - that court attorney or Referee may say, "I don't think my Judge would grant that," or "I don't think the odds are in your favor." In that case, you may want to come down off your posture a bit and rethink the position because otherwise, you may be spending a ton of money with little to no chance of getting the result you're looking for.

At this point, you and your attorney should have a very frank discussion about whether it is worth it to get to that point. As a client, ask yourself: is this an issue you want to spend $30-50,000+ pursuing? What if you have to budget out for a possible appeal from there, too?

This is one of the reasons why the court gets involved – to stop negotiations from reaching a stalemate on issues that wouldn't get favorably resolved in court anyway. After meeting with a Referee, court attorney, or Judge, you can often have a more pointed discussion about the rigidity of the settlement posture.

What Are the Steps in Negotiating A Contested Divorce Case?

Usually, the first step in negotiating a contested divorce is exchanging net worth statements on the financial issues. Exchanging net worth statements will aid the attorneys in knowing the incomes of both parties. It will also tell the attorneys what properties are involved, the total assets, and the total debts.

Once you have that net worth information, then one of three things usually happens:

1. The attorneys for both sides jump on the phone in an attorneys-only phone call,
2. One side or the other produces a settlement proposal letter or email, or

3. There's a four-way settlement conference.

It usually takes the parties anywhere from a few weeks to a few months to complete the net worth statements. In my humble opinion, however, completing the net worth statements should take, at most, a month as they're rather simple documents. If a party needs assistance along the way, s/he should reach out to the paralegal assigned to the case. After exchanging net worths, it may take anywhere from a few days to another month to exchange settlement positions and/or set up the four-way settlement conference.

The bottom line is the attorneys should have a good feel inside of four months to determine whether the case is settling or not. Under court rule, one is required to have the case settled within four months of the other side serving their answer to the complaint. If not, one is technically required to file for a contested divorce. No fixed penalty happens if the case can't settle within four months, but this policy (to file for a contested divorce in four months) is intended to move the case along.

Quite frankly, if the parties are not close to settling the case after four months of somewhat active negotiations, it doesn't do anyone any good to maintain the case as an uncontested. Presumably, the couples want to get divorced, and if your positions are still far apart, further negotiations at that point would not seem fruitful.

Is Some Flexibility Necessary to Successfully Negotiate In A Contested Divorce Case?

Flexibility is absolutely necessary to negotiate successfully in a contested divorce case. You do not want to negotiate by saying, "Here's my settlement position. I'm not willing to budge." It gives you truly little wiggle room. If one side or the other takes a rigid position, settlement negotiations are likely to be very short-lived.

As an attorney, you could go to the other side's counsel and say, "Look, here's my client's settlement position, and they haven't given me any authority for anything different. Is your client in agreement with that?" And if the other side says no, then it's best not to waste any more time. Contest the case and get a Judge involved.

Why Is Experience Negotiating Divorce and Other Family Law Related Matters So Critical In Contested Cases?

As of 2023, I have over 25 years of experience in New York Family Law matters. I was licensed as an attorney in March 1998 and have practiced family law almost exclusively ever since.

I briefly worked for a divorce law firm after I graduated from law school. I then became a family law prosecutor handling child support, child abuse, and child neglect cases for almost three years. I went into private practice in 2000, and at some point, around ten years into practice, my work became 100% percent family law.

Having that kind of experience helps because family law is the only thing I do all day, every day, week in, week out, month in, month out, year in, year out.

Of course, all attorneys must continue legal education, but suppose somebody is a general practice attorney and family law takes up 10, 20, or 30% of their practice. In that case, family law will also take up 10, 20, or 30% of their continued learning and education.

On the other hand, consider the sum of experience of an attorney who has practiced family law for 25 years and has *only* taken continuing legal education courses in family law.

I would respectfully say that the family law-focused attorney has much more experience in dealing with a contested family law case - as opposed to an attorney with 25 years of experience but who only spent 10-30% of their time in the family law field.

Having an attorney who only exclusively handles (or at least mostly handles) family law will result in the attorney having a ton more experience on the issues involved in your case.

CHAPTER 7

HOW IS CHILD CUSTODY DETERMINED IN NEW YORK?

It should be stated up front that most child custody cases in New York end up getting resolved with a settlement. That is, in most cases, the parties reach an agreement as to their custody arrangements and parenting plan outside of Court.

However, if we're getting to the core of this question, we're going to have to talk about what happens if there's no settlement in a custody case, and the matter needs to be decided by the Court.

In New York custody cases where the parties cannot reach an out-of-Court settlement (and thus have decided to pursue litigation), the Court is going to hear evidence and then analyze many issues (some of which may seem relatively minor).

For example, one such issue is often whether there is some allegation of a lack of parental unfitness on the part of one parent or the other. In this context, "unfitness" means that parent allegedly has something going on with them that precludes them from being a safe and responsible caretaker of their child. This could be a mental illness, anger management problems, a history of perpetrating domestic violence in the past or present, an issue with drugs or alcohol addiction, etc.

It's important to note that allegations of unfitness against one or both parents have to be proven. Parental unfitness cannot merely be assumed because someone (especially the other party in the custody case) says they suspect it's true. For example, the Court would not be able to declare parental unfitness of Parent X just because their co-parent said, "I think Parent X has a problem with drugs." This would not be sufficient evidence to prove the matter at trial.

Likewise, if there was an allegation of, say, drug problems against one parent, there has to be proof to use that issue to declare a lack of fitness for parenting. For sufficient proof, the alleging party would have to present evidence, such as pictures or video of the person being intoxicated, or perhaps a record of one or several DWI/DUI convictions (notably, these can only be brought as proof if they are convictions—merely being charged without being convicted is not enough evidence). If the parent with an alleged drug problem was sent to drug or alcohol rehab, you can request their rehab records through the Court, and present them as evidence as well.

Beyond unfitness issues, then the Court is going to look at the evidence to determine which parent is considered the "**primary psychological parent.**" This is an umbrella legalistic term for the parent who has performed the majority of the parenting tasks which go into raising a child up until the point of the separation or divorce.

Determining who is the **primary psychological parent** is a process that can consist of the court examining which parent is responsible for many different tasks. These include:

- Who gets the child or children up in the morning
- Who puts the child or children to bed at night
- Who feeds the child or children their meals
- Who prepares their meals for outside the home (i.e., lunch)
- Who gets them off to school
- Who makes sure they get home from school or are arranged for after school
- Who does homework with the children
- Who shops for the children's clothes
- Who arranges for playdates, actually takes them to the play date, and knows the children's friends (and their parents)
- Who arranges for medical or dental appointments
- Who takes the children to appointments
- Who participates in parent-teacher conferences

Like any other matter is proven in Court, claims regarding which parent does which task have to be documented with corroborating evidence. As such, you are generally going to need documentary evidence (or witness testimony) to corroborate the claims in order for it to have a meaningful chance of making a difference to the Court.

Beyond those two major issues, there's a bunch of other factors the Court takes into consideration in deciding on New York custody cases. These include:

- **The availability of each parent.** This is a matter that may seem obvious, but can sometimes become complicated. When trying to figure out which parent is more "available", the Court will consider how many hours in a given day they are usually physically present, as well as what kind of presence they can bring to their children. In many cases, though, it comes down to a matter of hours. For example, if one person is working 14 hours a day and the other has a 9:00-to-5:00 job and maybe works from home sometimes, then it's obvious which parent would be more available for the child

- **The nature, quality, and location of the home environments of each parent.** Assuming the parents are separated, the court will consider the nature and quality of the home environments of each parent. This includes issues like where each home is located (especially in relation to other things that are important to the child, like their school, their extracurricular activities, and their friend group); who else is residing with the child in the home (especially pertinent if there is someone who may pose a danger to the child); and whether the home is set up to properly house and facilitate healthy growth for the child.
- **The quality of care already provided by each parent.** The Court is also going to consider the quality of care the respective parents have already provided to the child or are providing to the child presently. This will be factored into the projected ability of both parents to care for the child going forward.

- **The stability of each parent**. The Court is also going to consider what level of stability is maintained in the life and person of each parent. In other words, how has the parent displayed their ability to provide a secure and stable foundation for the child? If one parent, for example, has bounced around 5 different houses in the last 5 years, and one parent has lived at the same house for the last 5 years, then there's a disparity there which can become a factor. This also refers to personal and interpersonal stability. Can each parent keep a level head and attend to their responsibilities on a regular basis? Are they refraining from bringing an undue amount of new or volatile people into the children's lives, especially if those people then disappear just as quickly? These are issues that are considered when determining custody, though certainly are not the be-all-and-end-all issues.
- **The preferences of the child (if applicable).** If the child is old enough to express a preference,

then the Court is going to consider the child's preferences, usually expressed through an attorney that's assigned to represent them, to a certain degree. However, it should be noted the weight given to a child's preferences varies significantly on a case-by-case basis. The primary guideline for the Judge is to act in the child's best interests. If they Judge finds the child's preference is not in their best interest otherwise, they will rule accordingly.

- **Parental alienation.** The Court will also consider issues of parental alienation. This is a tactic in which one parent violates the other parent's access rights or encourages the child to have negative associations with their other parent, or otherwise not to have a relationship with their other parent.
- **False accusation.** "False accusation" is where a parent has filed a false police report or a false child abuse or neglect report against their co-parent. In cases where the allegations were investigated and found to be false, those false accusations can be

presented before the Court as a factor for the Court to consider on custody matters.

- **Withholding of access.** This issue is similar to but not the same thing as parental alienation. It specifically refers to each parent's track record with adhering to and facilitating the custody and visitation arrangements made and set forth (whether formally or informally) thus far. The Judge will consider if one parent violates their co-parent's visitation rights (especially if doing so disregards Court Orders), or even if one parent is regularly and/or substantially late with pickups or drop-offs.
- **Involving a child in parent's conflict**. Unfortunately, parents sometimes lose sight of what is right when they are going through messy breakups. The end of a relationship is often painful and emotionally difficult, but it is imperative for parents to keep their children out of that emotional messiness as much as possible. If there is an accusation of involving the children in these conflicts by either parent

(preferably with documentation), it will be considered by the Court. Notably, this can be more insidious then just venting to a child inappropriately or making them take sides between parents. One example of more subtly involving a child in a parental conflict would be using the child as the messenger between the parents. I've had cases where the Father will give the child the child support check he owes, and then say, "Here, give this check to Mommy when you get back home cause she'll be asking for it." That is completely inappropriate and usually a factor the Court is going to consider.

- **Mental or emotional conditions.** The Court is also going to consider the mental or emotional stability of either parent, in addition to the physical stability of both parents and their homes. Obviously, this applies to serious mental illnesses such as schizophrenia and certain types of bipolar disorder, which while untreated make it impossible for the parents to care for themselves, never mind a child.

However, the Court is also going to consider any so-called "lesser mental illnesses", such as depression and anxiety, PTSD, and other things of that nature - to the degree it may affect parenting capacity.

- **Criminal convictions.** If either parent has any criminal convictions, this may be considered by the Court - though it is most pertinent if the convictions could endanger the child in any way. It is considered the most pertinent if the parent has any (e.g., convictions, charges, or indicative reports of child abuse or neglect, especially against the child or their siblings).
- **Moral character flaws.** Moral character flaws are hard to pin down exactly, but it essentially boils down to leading by example. Will the parent be able to lead by example when it comes to morality, based on their own behavior? Obviously, this is a rather subjective question, but if, say, one of the parents has an unaddressed gambling habit that has caused them to steal from their loved ones, and if they

primarily associate with other problem gamblers, then a question about their moral character may be raised. The same might be said about problem drinkers. Depending on the circumstances, these may be facts that the Court can consider.

- **The physical health of each parent.** Beyond any mental stability, mental health, or mental illness, there is also a question of whether either or both parents are physically well enough to be able to care for the child. This issue rarely comes into play but is theoretically a factor. For example, I've had some cases where the Father has been much older (perhaps in his 60s or 70s) than the mother (perhaps in her 30s or 40s). In those cases, the mother was usually much more physically able to keep up with the kids, and to be able to go out and play with them. This is not usually a major factor, but it very well might be a minor factor that the Court may take into consideration. I've also had cases where one parent or the other has had medical conditions where on unexpected occasions, they would pass out or become unresponsive, or have to be rushed to the hospital because of their medical issues. Certainly, it's not their fault they have such a condition, but it nevertheless would be a factor the Court would want to take into consideration. This is particularly true when addressing the question of a younger child living in their house the vast majority of the time.

- **Illegal conduct vis a vis the other party.** In some cases, divorces become fraught enough that one or both parties perpetrate illegal conduct against the other party. Some common examples may include stalking the other party, harassing the other party, violating Orders of Protection, tape recording of the other party without their consent (otherwise known as wiretapping), stealing the other party's property, and hacking into the other party's devices or accounts without their authorization. Illegal conduct perpetrated against the other party can be taken into consideration by the Court when determining custody.

- **The separation of siblings.** The Court often takes the family makeup/dynamic into consideration when deciding custody. This is especially true when it comes to siblings. Ideally, in most cases, the Court does not believe it is in the best interest of a child to separate them from their siblings. It is the tendency of the Court to try to keep closely bonded siblings together.
- **The disparate treatment of siblings or other relatives.** The Judge may consider if the child is treated differently from other siblings or relatives in the household, and if this may negatively affect their wellbeing. Importantly, this treatment doesn't have to come from the parent. It could come from any other relative or adult whom the parent regularly has in their home and/or in interaction with the child, including grandparents, aunts, uncles, and other family members (or significant others).
- **Inflexible parenting approaches.** This essentially means a behavior or attitude on the part of one parent which makes co-parenting

more difficult than necessary, or even impossible—and/or that seeks to avoid and impede cooperation with the co-parent—in a way demonstrably not in the child's best interest. An example of inflexible parenting is when one parent tries to mandate what the other parent does in their household, beyond issues of basic health and safety. Perhaps one parent eats organic food, and the other parent doesn't really care one way or the other about organic food. If the one parent dictates to their co-parent they *have to* feed the child organic food when the child is under the co-parent's roof, this may be considered inflexible parenting.

- **Obsessive medical treatment.** In some custody cases, there is a recurrent issue in which one parent may be seeking undue medical care and treatment for their child. In my experience, this issue usually comes from a custodial parent who's trying to alienate the child from the non-custodial parent. Nevertheless, the Judge may consider whether a parent is determined there is something "wrong" with the child despite being told the child is healthy—especially when they are trying to prove "damage" from neglect or abuse by the other parent. An example of obsessive medical treatment of this sort is "doctor shopping" (i.e., going from one doctor or one child counselor to another until they get one who agrees with their stance).

- **Moves or relocations.** Moving is sometimes part of a parent or family's life, and is sometimes necessary to tend to work, family, or financial needs. However, there are certain moves by custodial parents which may have the implicit intention of interfering with the other parent's custody/visitation rights or their relationship with the child. One example is if the custodial parent moved the child far enough away that it would be impossible for the non-custodial parent to access their visitation and custody rights. If this has indeed occurred, it can be considered a display of bad faith on the part of the custodial parent in their continued willingness to facilitate any Court-Ordered visitation.

- **Financial ability to care for the child.** The financial situation of both parties is also a factor in custody decisions to a limited extent. It should be noted it is usually a minor factor only because whichever parent gets custody will be able to claim s/he (even if they make substantially less than the other parent) would receive child support as well. In this way, financial ability can be considered a kind of "muted factor."
- **Voluntary agreements.** This factor only applies in cases where the parties had already worked out some kind of agreement or schedule, even informally, about how parenting responsibilities, scheduling, and custody were going to work before they went to the Court to resolve the matter. The way these agreements are considered has a lot to do with whether objections were raised, and whether documentation can be presented by the objecting party attesting to their objection.
- **Educational Issues.** Another factor the court is going to take into consideration is the education of the children, as well as any educational issues

which may arise if either parent was to have a custody decision ruled in their favor. Often, this becomes relevant where there is a major disagreement between the parents about schooling, wherein one parent wants to send the children to one type of school and the other parent disagrees. It also becomes relevant in homeschooling cases, in which the children were primarily homeschooled by one parent. It may also include consideration about the contributions and support each parent provides to the child's academic life, and to their continued growth and success in school, as well as their school's community.

- **Intentionally misleading the Court.** If either party has actual evidence the other party misled the Court in any way—up to and including perjury—they should definitely present it to the Court as soon as possible. Specifically, you can attempt to bring forth rebuttal evidence or witnesses to rebut the false or misleading evidence or testimony.

While this list of factors may seem comprehensive, it is definitely not exhaustive. Depending on your case, different factors will obviously be given different degrees of weight in the ultimate decision of the Court.

What Are Some Of The Reasons Why Custody Arrangements Become Contested Matters?

Custody arrangements usually become contested matters when there is a sharp divide in terms of what the parents want—usually when it comes to one parent wanting the child or children to live with them, versus the other parent wanting the child or children to live with them.

For example, we often try to work out shared custody in the pre-trial negotiation phases. If the parties don't want to do shared custody or don't deem it to be feasible—perhaps because of issues like the geographical distance between the parents—the parties can attempt to work out divisions of time that would come as close as possible to shared custody.

Ultimately, though, if the parents find themselves unwilling or unable to agree, and if each parent can't see themselves agreeing to anything within the ballpark of what the other parent is asking for, then custody cases will usually have to go to Court.

What Happens When Parents Cannot Agree on a Child Custody Arrangement?

As stated above, the parents (through their attorneys and with the aid of the Court, and potentially mediators, facilitators, or counselors) do whatever they can to attempt to negotiate an agreement. One should consider whether they believe both want full physical custody, or whether they are willing to entertain the idea of shared custody. One should consider options like an 8-6 split (where one parent has 8 nights, and the other parent has 6 nights), or a 9-5 split (where one parent has 9 nights, and the other parent has 5 nights) over the course of a 14-day (or two week) spread.

At times, permutations in parenting time are necessary not because of disagreement between the parties, but because of logistical issues. For example, I just settled a custody case where the mother and the father lived around 30 miles apart, and therefore true shared custody (exactly 50%-50% time) was not feasible, especially during the school year.

In cases like that – and where the parties still wish to share custody - we can zoom out from a 14-day spread, and instead pose things in terms of a full year, a 365-day calendar. We can use this as a framework to better and more feasibly maximize each parent's time with the child. With this framework, we could design the schedule to give, for instance, the mother more time with the children during the school year, and then make up additional time for the father on long weekends, school breaks, holidays, and summer vacation.

Ultimately, at the end of the day, if you walk through every theoretical permutation of access and the parties continue to insist they don't want any of those options, then the only other choice is to contest.

What Components Of Co-Parenting Should Parents Agree On When It Comes To A Custody Arrangement?

There are some guideline examples often cited as things which should be agreed on when it comes to custody arrangements. This includes things that experts believe should be consistent between households, like vaccines, healthcare, or religion.

In theory, though, parents should strive to reach an agreement on all the major issues in a child's life. The agreement negotiation process, and even the Court litigation process, is there to help parents make those decisions when they disagree.

Quite obviously, if two parents are able to reach an agreement on an issue—especially on major issues—then they don't really need lawyers (perhaps just a mediator). They don't need the Court, other than to perhaps just sign off on an Order incorporating the agreement they have already reached.

For example, I've had parties come to me at the initial consultation and say, "Guess what? We largely don't need you because we've reached an agreement on all the basic terms, and here it is." Then they write up the basic terms, and then it's just a matter of my office drafting the formal Stipulation, filing the Petition in Court, and then going before the Judge. At that point, all I have to say is, "Judge, good news. We settled the case already. Here is the Stipulation. We just need an Order."

Of course, that's not the vast majority of cases that I handle. In about 98 to 99% of cases that I handle, the parties are not able to reach agreements on certain issues (at least not on their own) and we have to do at least some sort of mediation or negotiation process, and – if negotiation is unsuccessful - Court litigation.

I have seen lately there is quite a bit of disagreement between co-parents with respect to COVID vaccines. This has become a sort of "hot-button issue" in 2022, so I'd like to say a little bit more about it here.

While it might be different in other states (such as Florida), in New York, there's strong public policy supporting the vaccination of children and adults. As a parent, if you object to the vaccine but your co-parent wants the children vaccinated, you have to face the prospect of going before a Court that is ultimately going to base their determination on science, which will affect the outcome.

And while I might have my personal views on the issue, that doesn't affect how I represent a particular client. If I have a client that objects to the vaccine, I'm not going to bring my personal beliefs into it. Instead, the party objecting to the COVID vaccine will need to come forth with the actual medical proof—preferably from a licensed medical doctor in the state of New York who would ultimately be willing to testify to the Court that they do not recommend the vaccine for children.

Of course, one would probably be hard-pressed to find such a doctor in New York, and I would venture a guess the other side would be able to find far more doctors who would testify or submit documentary evidence that the vaccine is recommended for children.

At the end of the day, though, this is a decision for the Judge to make, and you have the right to gather whatever evidence you can and present it to the Judge.

What Are Some Less Discussed But Still Important Components Of Co-Parenting?

There are many different decisions that go into co-parenting, and many components of a cooperative co-parenting relationship.

One example is whether a child should do a particular activity, and how that activity may or may not conflict with the child's set schedule. For example, let's say Parent X wants the child to play baseball, and Parent Y wants the child to play piano. Let's say in this case the league Parent X wants the child to play baseball on has practices and games that conflict with Parent Y's proposed piano lessons.

Conflicts like this are usually very hard for either an attorney or a Judge to weigh in on. In all likelihood, if there's a conflict like this, the Judge will probably say it isn't their job to dictate which particular activities the child does when the child is in each house.

So, if parents can't make the decision amongst themselves, they may find themselves in a situation where the child goes to baseball practice when they're in the custody of Parent X and goes to piano lessons when they're in the custody of Parent Y. If those two activities happen at the same time, then the child will wind up not being able to participate in either activity fully, and will miss out. They will be at a disadvantage compared to their peers, who either go to every piano lesson or every baseball practice. This is obviously not in the best interest of the child, which is usually enough to motivate the parents to come to some sort of agreement. Still, this is an example of where parents' disagreement would potentially be hurting their own child.

Hopefully, in an instance like the baseball/piano conflict, there would be some level of give and take and some degree of compromise. For example, the child could attend piano lessons when baseball isn't in season. While this may seem like an obvious solution, some parents in the midst of an argument may not see it as obvious.

Another example is if the child has friends where Parent X lives, but no friends where Parent Y lives. If the child is getting older and wants to spend more time alone with their peers, the child may say they want to spend more time at Parent X's house—not to spend more time with Parent X, but to be able to spend time with their friends. This sort of thing is also very difficult for an attorney or Judge to adjudicate, and therefore really needs to be solved between the parents.

Are There Some Things That Should Not be Discussed between Co-Parents?

The day-to-day activities of the child, barring activities that pose demonstrable harm to the child, would not need to be discussed between co-parents (by which I mean, would not have to be decided in the course of a child custody case).

I have had instances in which one or both parents have tried to dictate the behavior of the other parent in their own home, under the guise that they were trying to discuss the activities of the child. For example, I had one parent say that they knew for a fact the other parent was allowing their 11-year-old child to watch PG-13 movies.

An issue like this is not a bright line test. Every parent can decide for themselves whether they let their child watch PG-13 movies. Just because the Motion Pictures Association of America decides that a twelve-year-old shouldn't watch a particular movie doesn't necessarily mean any parent is mandated to agree with the MPAA's decision. That's where the disconnect comes in, especially when people are looking for a reason to start a custody fight because of interpersonal acrimony – they tend to heighten recommendations or guidelines into rigid rules.

I've had other parents say they want to mandate a certain bedtime for the child in both houses. They may tell me they *know* the other parent allows the child to stay up until midnight, which means the child goes to school tired the next day.

While this may be true, you really need some sort of proof to back up the allegation – i.e., staying up late is definitely bad for the child, or causes the child to be tired the next day to their detriment. Different kids need different amounts of sleep, and sometimes parents just make assumptions without actually asking the child – much less their teachers or pediatrician.

Again, parents who are in a highly emotional and contested custody battle may be more likely to view things as harmful which aren't totally harmful. They may begin to adopt their own notions of parenting as the golden rule of parenting that must be accepted between households, such as bedtimes, choice of food, choice of movies or TV, or other things along those lines. These are, more often than not, issues a Judge will refuse to get into or rule on, unless there's some clear evidence the child is being harmed.

For example, if we are going with the accusation of staying up too late on school nights, the Judge would really have to hear this from the child's teacher. The teacher would have to clearly testify that on days after the child is with their father (for example), the child comes to school exhausted to the point where they aren't functioning (e.g., slumped over their desk and sleeping). If you have that sort of evidence, then you might have something to build on with the Judge.

What Is Crucial to Be Mindful of When Communicating with My Child's Other Parent in a Contested Custody Case?

It's best to focus on the particular issues at hand rather than the communication style or the history of conflict you have with the other parent. Bringing up events of the past is marching down the wrong road. Instead, you want to stay as objective as possible. With any relationship, especially where parties are going through a contested custody situation, there is bitterness, hurt feelings, and a history that is not easily forgotten. When parties communicate, they tend to hold grudges and use details from the past in current arguments.

If this happens and the other parent is bringing up details from your history, do not try to address it or confront them. If you do so, you are just going to have arguments at that point which will delay solving the issue.

There are many cases where the other parent is overbearing or perhaps narcissistic. They may even have diagnosable psychological disorders that get in the way of effective co-parenting and communication. One should remain as objective as possible and manage boundaries. For example, if the other parent sends 5, 6, or 10 emails a day, don't feel obligated to respond to each one. If it makes sense to respond, do so, but never under the assumption that you are obligated to email back. Instead, prioritize deciphering the sum and substance of the emails.

Some people run into the issue of not having time to read 10 emails a day if the other parent is emailing. If you don't feel like reading them, especially at the end of a long workday, get a Dictaphone app on your iPhone or Android device to turn those texts into audio. You can sit and listen to them on the commercial break of your favorite show. Listening to emails like this can also remove some of the hostility in communicating with an aggressive parent.

What Happens If Two Parties Are Unable To Effectively Communicate In A Contested Custody Case?

When you have already tried emailing, texting, a program such as Our Family Wizard, Talking Parents, or 2 Houses and still can't effectively communicate, mediation is the typical option, otherwise known as parenting coordinator. Mediation costs money but will cost less if you have two separate lawyers and are going into court before a Judge. I may recommend this option first if there are no sharply contested issues, domestic violence, mental health issues, etc.

If I have a client that simply cannot communicate with the other parent, even in writing, then it's not a case where joint custody is workable. This is because joint custody assumes the parents are going to be able to effectively communicate, even if only in writing.

What Happens When a Custody Case Ends Up Going to Trial?

In New York, custody trials take place over 3 to 5 (or more) trial dates. Sometimes they are just morning blocks of time, sometimes they are all day blocks, and sometimes they are just afternoon blocks. Generally, they are periods of about 1 to 3 hours in which you will work with your attorney to establish evidence and witnesses. The Judge will want confirmation at the pretrial conference - or a certain amount of time thereafter - to have an exhibit and witness list. Therefore, you should already plan with your attorney for this. What documents, what videos, what texts, and what emails do we want going into our exhibit list? Do we need to subpoena any persons or documents? If so, let's get that going. What witnesses do we want on our direct case? What witnesses do we want to hold off for a possible rebuttal to evidence that may be put forth against us?

You shouldn't wait until you select trial dates and then start having these discussions with your attorney. Sometimes it is already too late to start mounting an effective case if you wait until trial dates have already been set because now you are scrambling trying to get witnesses lined up and subpoenas out. It is important to note that there are sometimes issues and delays when getting responses to subpoenas.

Can a Custody Case Still Be Settled Outside of Court Even If We're Already in the Middle of a Trial?

Yes. The courts always encourage settlements even in the middle of a trial. The parents can and should keep talking with each other if there are no orders of protection in place or injunctions.

If the parents are in the middle of a trial, that means they tried to settle the case with every settlement permutation the attorneys and the court can think of, but it hasn't happened. While it is possible that cases can settle in the middle of the trial, it becomes increasingly unlikely once a trial actually begins.

CHAPTER 8

CHILD SUPPORT IN A CONTESTED CASE

What Information Must Be Disclosed By Each Parent When It Comes To Determining Support Obligations And

If you are in family court, each parent needs to submit a financial disclosure affidavit, the last filed tax return, usually a current and/or representative pay stubs along with tax returns. Each parent is also supposed to submit their W-2s and 1099s which were filed with the tax return.

However, if you're in a Supreme Court on a divorce matter, then you submit a "net worth statement" instead of the financial disclosure affidavit. There's also a whole broad range of documents and information that is discretionary which can be exchanged or ordered to be exchanged by the court.

How Is Child Support Assigned And Calculated in New York State?

Child support is pursuant to the Child Support Standards Act. The income of both parents must be calculated. For each parent's income calculation, there are a few routine deductions from gross income for child support: FICA, Medicare tax, and the respective city tax. This arrives at "adjusted gross income." The parents' income is then combined to arrive at combined parental income.

Then the following percentages for child support calculation are applied to the parents' combined income:

- 17% for one child

- 25% for two children
- 29% for three children
- 31% for four children
- 35% for five or more children

For example, if the dad makes two-thirds of the combined parental income and the mom makes one third, that's the proportionate share. An illustration follows in Table 1:

Table 1: Non-Custodial Child Support Payment Chart

Parents	Income less deductions	Combined Income	% of combined income	No. of Children	Amount of Child Support required for non-custodial parent
				1 Child @ 17%	
Dad	$63,360	$96,000	66%	11.22%	$10,000
Mom	$31,680		33%	5.61%	$5,386
				2 Children @ 25%	
Dad	$63,360	$96,000	66%	16.5%	$15,840
Mom	$31,680		33%	8.25%	$7,920
				3 Children @ 29%	
Dad	$63,360	96,000	66%	19.14%	$18,374
Mom	$31,680		33%	9.57%	$9,158

In New York State, it is only the non-custodial parent (the parent the children do not live with) who actually pays child support. In the above table, if the dad was the non-custodial parent, he would pay $10,771 a year for one child, which is about $898 a month. If the mom was the non-custodial parent, she would pay $5,386 a year for one child, which is $449 a month. The only thing a custodial parent would pay is if the non-custodial parent happens to incur any add-on expenses such as health insurance, medical expenses, educational costs, and child care.

What Are Some of the Most Common Reasons Why Child Support Or Spousal Support is Contested?

One of the common reasons support issues are contested is "income." There can be many reasons why a parent's income is deemed inaccurate. One example is if a party has self-employment income. Likewise, if the parent owns a business, it may be highly subjective what the parent actually makes (as opposed to what s/he claims on taxes). There could also be a host of financial disclosures which would need to take place if the parent owns a business.

Another common reason could be the person has on-the-books income versus off-the-books income. A lot of financial disclosures would need to be submitted to arrive at the parent's true income.

Yet another way child support could be contested is when one child lives with mom and the other child lives with dad. Then you have to calculate who pays what for each child.

Another way child support could be contested is the **"Above the Cap" Calculations**. In other words, as of 2022 under New York State law, one calculates combined parental income up to the statutory cap of $163,000. The law does adjust the cap once every two years based on the CPI index, which means that the statutory cap might go up by about $5,000 to $10,000 each two years. But cases aren't contested based on parental income below $163,000.

With high income cases, the court may decide on a cap of $250,000, or $300,000 or $350,000, or $400,000. Or the court doesn't use a cap at all. There are cases where the court went up as high as $600,000 to $800,000 in combined parental income.

If The Amount Of Child Support Is A Set Calculation, How Can Anyone Contest These Matters?

While child support is a set calculation, arriving at the combined parental income is not as simple as doing your taxes. For example, just because somebody says, "My tax return states I made $80,000 last year" doesn't mean they did. Child support payment calculations are not the same. The court will expect you to prove your income, much like an IRS audit. The court may want to see your W-2s and 1099s, in addition to your expenses if you don't take the standard deduction but file the long form.

If you have business expenses on your individual tax return (via your Schedule C), or a corporate tax return, the other parent is entitled to see the supporting documents. Thus, actual income less allowed expenses and including business earnings can cause the amount of child support to be contested.

For example, the court (or opposing counsel) might say, "In addition to seeing your bank statements, we also want to see the receipts and invoices for your business expenses because we want to be able to make sure they are legitimate business expenses." Even the IRS audits individual taxes because people deduct the expense of personal meals, personal rent, or a portion thereof. They'll claim their personal car as a company car and use that as a deduction on a tax return. People even deduct their personal utilities and claim them as business utilities. This happens more often when people operate businesses out of their own houses.

Another item to explore is if you say you have a business, where do you operate that business? If it's operated out of your basement and you're claiming your electric bill as the business expense and taking it as a deduction, that would be a deduction for child support purposes. However, how can you prove you are paying the electric bill - and what portion is attributable to your business versus your personal use?

These examples are some of the many issues that show how parental income can be contested and further explored in pretrial disclosure.

What Happens If The Parent Who's Required To Pay Fails To Pay Child Support In New York State? How Does New York Generally Enforce Child Support Payments?

It depends on whether the child support was paid through a support collection unit. The support collection unit is a state agency that collects child support on behalf of the custodial parent. If the non-custodial parent falls behind and support is paid through the support collection unit, then that unit has many different powers.

Here are some of the ways the support collection unit can require the non-custodial parent to pay:

- Suspend the person's licenses, including a driver's license
- Seize tax return refunds
- Go after a person's bank accounts and assets
- Seize other types of assets
- Garnish wages

If the initial support case is not paid through the support collection unit, the custodial parent -

often in conjunction with their own attorney - needs to take all those actions themselves. In other words, they need to file a violation case with the court, and seek to hold the non-custodial parent in willful violation of the child support.

When the non-custodial parent is found in willful violation, the court has many different powers. They include a money judgment that would include 9% interest on the unpaid child support payments in addition to the list above. The support payee can take that judgment and use income from property, assets, money in the bank, retirement, and investments to pay the child support.

If the custodial parent did not have the support paid through the support collection unit, they can request that at the violation stage, so the support collection unit can aid in their efforts to collect the amount of support owed.

If the Parents Can't Agree on All the Terms of Child Support, What Are the Most Productive Ways to Resolve These Types of Matters?

The most productive way is through negotiation and having a sit-down with the parent to say, "Does it make sense to spend many thousands or tens of thousands of dollars taking the particular issue to trial, or is there a way to compromise and agree?"

For example, if the issue is should we extend child support beyond the age of 21 if the child's going to college? Sometimes you get push back from the non-custodial parent because they see such a statement as the custodial parent's lucky break. In effect, they say "The child's clearly an adult at that point. I have no problem paying for college, but I do have a problem continuing to pay basic child support for a child that's 22 years old."

There's a way to compromise. The court cannot mandate (unless the child is disabled) any child support including payment for college beyond age 21. However, one way to resolve that issue is to discuss whether child support gets cut-off when the child finishes the spring semester after the child turns 21. This would prevent child support from stopping the month of February, making it difficult to finish college.

But the other way that you can compromise is on the amount of basic child support. So again, using the example of a child's turning 21, still in college but the non-custodial parent says, "I want to continue paying basic support beyond age 21. I have no problem paying for college." You could also have the agreement saying that basic support will terminate at age 21. But both parents' contributions to college will continue beyond age 21 until the child either finishes their 4-year college education or at some point fixed earlier. You could even put in a particular date. You could say, "Well, I'll continue paying until May of 2034." These are ways to resolve the issue of what happens to support when the child turns 21.

Does Child Support Have to Be Resolved And/Or Finalized Before a Divorce Will Be Granted in New York State?

The answer is yes - child support needs to be resolved. You can have it in the settlement agreement that where there's a family court case pending, child support will be resolved in the pending case (thus, you will not be resolving it in the divorce case itself, but in family court). Or you have to have a provision that says the parents are aware of what the guidelines are now, but they're agreeing to either defer child support now for some specific reason stated in the agreement (and approved by the court), or they set an amount. But one of those scenarios needs to be in the divorce settlement or else it is not going to be approved by the divorce judge. Nevertheless, in most cases, the amount of child support is stated within the divorce judgment.

CHAPTER 9

CONTESTED FAMILY LAW CASES: CONCLUDING REMARKS

Will my Case Actually End up being Contested and/or Go To Trial?

Divorce and other family law matters often proceed to trial due to custody and significant financial issues. In such cases, clients may be hesitant to reach a settlement due to the potentially high cost of a trial. The expense of a trial can reach up to $30,000-50,000+, with a typical financial trial consisting of two to three trial dates, each lasting approximately seven hours.

Clients should also anticipate one to two hours of billable time for every hour spent in court.

Thus, if the difference between the two parties on child support or alimony is not substantial, it may not be worthwhile to go to trial. In the event of custody disputes, settling the matter outside of court by exploring every possible permutation is essential. By engaging in discussions to consider access time and other variables, clients can avoid a trial and reduce legal fees.

Joint custody is an additional issue that often arises in custody disputes, and it rarely leads to litigation. As discussed above, parents can use various applications such as Family Wizard, Talking Parents, or 2 Houses to facilitate communication regarding joint custody issues without direct contact with the other parent. This approach can provide an effective way to avoid the high costs of a trial.

In some cases, a client may be at risk of losing physical custody of their child. To prevent this outcome, legal counsel may suggest offering a midweek visit or two, sharing access time over the summer, school breaks, and holidays. Clients should consider this option instead of paying higher legal fees for a trial, especially when the outcome is uncertain.

Preparing For Trial

Preparing a client for trial is a crucial aspect of family law practice. To start, if there is a possibility of custody being contested, we send out a custody questionnaire, factor charts, and event timeline to the client[12].

The custody questionnaire is a detailed document that provides us with as much information and background on the parties as possible. It includes a skeleton in the closet questionnaire to ensure that we are not caught off guard at trial. Once the client completes the questionnaire, we schedule an appointment to go over it together.

---

[12] Checkout my book "Navigating Your New York Post-Divorce Case" for the Custody Timeline & Factor Charts. You'll find the Custody Questionnaire in my forthcoming book "Navigating Your New York Contested Custody Case.

The custody factor chart is also a critical document as it constitutes every conceivable factor that the court considers on a contested custody determination. We have separate columns where the client fills in all the positive and negative factors on their end, as well as the other side's.

Similarly, for financial issues, we prepare asset distribution charts[13], maintenance distribution charts, and child support variance charts. These documents lay out all the statutory factors and allow the client to provide relevant facts and circumstances for both positive and negative factors on their end and the opposing party.

Additionally, we ask the client to fill in an event timeline, including all relevant events and any corroborating evidence such as emails, text messages, videos, or audios. This timeline ensures that we have a comprehensive understanding of the case's history and

---

[13] See Appendix A for the Asset Distribution Chart.

can form a script of the direct examination and presentation of the direct case.

It is essential to prepare for trial as early as possible and not wait until trial dates are set. In my practice, I start preparing for a trial as soon as I perceive the possibility of a contested issue. Although it is ultimately up to the client to complete the documents, we encourage them to fill them out early on in the case to ensure that we have all the relevant information to present the strongest case possible.

What to Expect During Trial

It is crucial to provide clients with an estimate of the potential costs involved. This will allow them to make an informed decision about whether they wish to proceed with a trial or explore alternative options.

In addition, it is important for clients to understand the factors that the court will consider in their case. To this end, factor charts on asset distribution, maintenance, child support variance, and child custody should be provided. These charts outline the various factors that will be considered by the court and enable clients to better understand the strengths and weaknesses of their case.

Furthermore, it is essential for clients to be actively involved in the preparation process for trial. You can do this by filling out the factor charts and event timeline, which will result in a better understanding of the strengths and weaknesses of your case.

You should refer to **Appendix B** in this book for the Trial Testimony Instructions my office provided to clients - included in the form is a sample direct testimony script.

Preparation For Every Divorce And Other Family Law Case Is Unique

Each family law case is unique and requires a tailored approach. For example, if a client retains legal services for an uncontested case, the preparation approach will differ from that of a contested case. In the latter scenario, where the client anticipates that the case is likely to go to trial, a thorough preparation approach is necessary to ensure that the client is well-equipped for the possibility of a trial.

In summary, a nuanced approach is necessary for each case, which takes into account the unique circumstances of the case and the needs and goals of the client. A commitment to working closely with clients to ensure they are well-informed and well-prepared throughout the trial process is essential.

It is important to remember that trials are not as simple as presenting a document to a judge and letting them make a decision. Testimony and documentary evidence must be presented for each of the 16 statutory factors on equitable distribution, even for a "relatively simple case." Thus, when taking any case to trial, it is essential to weigh the costs and benefits and determine whether it makes financial sense to spend money on an attorney to take the disputed issue to trial.

The Final Decision in A Contested Divorce Matter

In a contested divorce matter, it is always the client who makes the final decision on settlement or whether to take the case to trial.

But while the client determines the settlement terms and whether or not to proceed to trial, the attorney advises on the law, the odds of winning, and the strengths or weaknesses of the case on individual issues.

Appealing a Judge's Decision

In a contested divorce case, all decisions made by a judge after trial are presumptively appealable provided that they are incorporated into a final order or judgment of divorce. Even if you feel that there is a solid basis to do so, you can possibly file a motion to renew or re-argue the decision. All decisions are final only at the trial level but are subject to the ability to appeal or file a motion to renew.

In Summation

I sincerely hope this book assists you in the preparation of your contested divorce - or contested Family Court - case.

My best piece of advice is: don't think you can go it alone. This book isn't meant to take the place of a lawyer - quite the opposite: it's intended to assist you in (a) knowing what to expect and (b) helping your lawyer better prepare you for trial.

If you cannot afford counsel, consider requesting the Judge assign you an attorney. Assigned Counsel are available to indigent persons[14] in New York family law cases. You may also contact the Court's Office of the Self-Represented – they may be able to get you a pro bono lawyer or at least a consultation with one.

You can also shop around for a lawyer – different lawyers charge different rates. And if your case is pending in an expensive county (e.g., Manhattan or Westchester), consider shopping for lawyers in adjoining counties (who may charge less due to the lower costs of running a practice in, say Queens vis-à-vis Manhattan).

---

14 https://www.ils.ny.gov/files/Blackletter%20with%20Commentary%20021621.pdf.

If you're unsure of whether or not to hire an attorney, *at the very least* please schedule a consultation with one! Then make an informed decision from there as to whether you wish to try it on your own.

I wish you all the best!

APPENDIX A

ASSET/PROPERTY DISTRIBUTION FACTOR CHART

One should list all information which you feel is arguably relevant to each factor. List <u>both</u> information which *supports* your claims/defenses in the case, as well as information which you think may hurt the opposing party's claims/defenses in the case. <u>All entries should be supported with references to documentary and/or witness evidence (& copies of same should be provided to our office on or before the Pre-Trial Conference at the latest) – if it is not, you risk the Court not accepting your mere testimony as sufficient evidence of the factor</u>.

1. The income and property of each party (a) at the time of the marriage, <u>and</u> (b) at the time of the commencement of the action (e.g., did a spouse get rid of assets or property? Did a party increase/decrease income in the months leading up to the divorce? Is the other party hiding income, property, or other assets? Did

the other party acquire assets/property post-commencement, but with "marital" funds? Is either party making a claim for "separate property/assets" being contributed to the marital pie and/or credits which either party feels entitled to?

2. The duration of the marriage and the age and health of both parties
3. The need of a custodial parent [of minor children] to occupy or own the marital residence and to use or own its household effects (i.e., is one party asking to remain in the house for a period of time before the sale/buy-out – and if so, for how long & why?)
4. The loss of inheritance and pension (or other retirement assets) rights upon dissolution of the marriage as of the date of the dissolution (e.g., is either party due a distribution from an estate? Did either party take a loan/withdrawal from a retirement account? If so, when & how much – and where did that money go? Are there trust funds?)

5. The loss of health insurance benefits upon dissolution of the marriage (i.e., is either party covered on the other's medical insurance & unable to get their own insurance?)
6. Any award of maintenance under Domestic Relations Law, Section 236-B(6)
7. Any equitable claim to, interest in, or direct or indirect contribution made to the acquisition of such marital property by the party not having a title, including joint efforts or expenditures and contributions and services as a spouse, parent, wage earner, and homemaker, and to the career or career potential of the other party (e.g., was a degree or license earned during the marriage? If yes, what value did it add to that spouse's career? Did 1 party care for the kids a lot more than the other party? If yes, detail such efforts. If one party owns a business, did the other party perform any work or other assistance to that business? If yes, detail.
8. The liquid or non-liquid character of all marital property (i.e., is one party requesting a cash

pay-out of the assets, rather than, say, a QDRO on the retirement or an exchange of property? If yes, what are the reasons?)

9. The probable future financial circumstances of each party (do you think you & your spouse's foreseeable economic future will stay about the same as it is now, go substantially up in the next few years, or go substantially down in the next few years? If a big change is anticipated, provide the reasons why)
10. The impossibility or difficulty of evaluating any component asset or any interest in a business, corporation, or profession, and the economic desirability of retaining such asset or interest intact and free from any claim or interference by the other party (e.g., does one party own a business, a professional practice or license or some other complex asset which isn't easily about to fix a value upon?)
11. The tax consequences to each party (after consultation with an accountant or financial advisor, is client aware of any particular tax

impacts to various settlement proposals being considered?)

12. The wasteful dissipation of assets by either spouse (e.g., gambling, reckless spending, spending money on a paramour, drug use, mismanagement of assets or rental properties, draining funds to pay for one's "own purposes" while ignoring joint/marital expenses, ignoring pleas to put property on the market when the property was a cash drain, committing tax fraud, etc.)
13. Any transfer or encumbrance made in contemplation of a matrimonial action without fair consideration (e.g., giving money or property to a friend or relative somewhat close to the divorce filing just to "get rid of it," stashing money or other assets in a trust or other hidden account, etc.)
14. Whether either party has committed an act or acts of domestic violence, against the other party and the nature, extent, duration, and impact of such act or acts:

15. In awarding the possession of a companion animal, the court shall consider the best interest of such animal. If applicable, please specify what facts you believe are relevant
16. Any other facts/factor(s) which you think the court should consider (e.g., did a spouse manipulate his/her career or lifestyle in order to dissipate assets or income potential? Was a party financially irresponsible?)

___

Regarding the Marital Residence:

Who lives in the house now:

___

Who wishes to live in the house after the divorce:

___

Comments regarding proposals for distribution of property:

___

Rationale, if any, for not distributing assets 50%-50%:

____

Factual basis for claims, if any, for distribution from spouse's separate (pre-marital, gifted, inherited, etc.) assets:

____

Factual basis for claims, if any, for allocation to spouse of marital debts (credit cards, etc.):

____

<u>REMINDER</u>: If you would like the attorney to subpoena documents and/or witnesses for trial, such subpoenas should generally be issued more than 30 days prior to your court date to allow sufficient time for the production of the records/witness - and generally you must include an advance payment for each subpoena in order to cover disbursements associated therewith.

Clients should produce to their attorney at least 30 days in advance of trial current & representative copies of all statements, bills, invoices, etc.

corroborating each & every item recorded on the client's Net Worth Statement (income, expenses, assets & debts) if this hasn't already been done.

APPENDIX B

GENERAL TESTIMONY INSTRUCTIONS – TRIAL

Testimony will be conducted in a question-and-answer format. First I will ask questions of you, and this is called "direct examination." Then each opposing attorney (or opposing party if self-represented) will be allowed to question you – that's called "cross-examination."

You should always testify truthfully. Understand the question and think about each answer before answering. Answer only the question asked (do not volunteer information). Do not guess. Avoid stating matters as absolutes. Seek to review any document which would refresh your recollection if you're unsure of the answer – but first state "I don't recall." Answer every question completely but as simply as possible. You should be polite and not argue with the person questioning you – but if it's opposing counsel, you should stand your ground and not try to be their friend or "help them out" by guessing as to the "real meaning" of his/her question.

Make sure to review a copy of your pleadings & replies thereto, as well as any affidavits you've submitted in this case. You should re-review these documents before each & every appearance. You should also be familiar with the other party's pleadings and affidavits so you know how best to respond on cross-examination. If applicable, you should thoroughly review all internal questionnaire forms, timelines, and factor charts – I recommend to study such items and notes for trial like you would for a big college exam so that your testimony flows as smoothly as possible.

Additionally, you should familiarize yourself with your key financial documents, especially those which either we – or the opposing side – has identified as potential trial exhibits. It is common, for example, for the opposing attorney to ask about particular charges on particular dates reflecting on credit card statements, particular deposits or withdrawals from bank account statements, particular entries on your tax returns, and/or particular entries on your net worth statement(s). You should familiarize yourself enough with each document so as to be prepared to answer questions regarding them. You may also take notes based on the documents - and if you forget particular entries on those documents, you may state, "I cannot recall, can I refresh my recollection?" The Judge will usually allow you to then refresh your recollection based on a review of your notes - with the proviso that the opposing side may then also request to see those notes.

You should stop testifying if an attorney objects (or the opposing party if s/he is representing themselves) and listen to the objection. If you are giving direct testimony and the Judge states "sustained," that means you cannot answer. If the Judge says "overruled," then you can. The reverse is true if you're answering questions on cross-examination.

Avoid exaggerated body language and intense emotion unless the topic calls for it (e.g., the death of a loved one). You should get a good night's sleep before testimony and inform me about any medication you must take before or after your testimony. You should appear clean and wear clean, neat clothing that is not "flashy" or "loud."

Treat all persons, including the opposing party, with respect. Consider this a solemn occasion.

Please bear in mind the following considerations:

- concise, objective, and factual responses have the most credibility;
- objectivity is enhanced with brevity, precise articulation, a slight formality, no expression of feelings, and a willingness to correct oneself and ask for clarifying questions;
- parties who trust the system's fairness will present themselves better;
- parties who distrust the system will appear arrogant, stiff, fearful, or cowed;

- a witness should not be frightened of disapproval and should accept criticism with poise;
- counterfeit sincerity or overstated feelings usually can be recognized.
- Never lose your temper;
- Speak slowly and clearly;
- If you don't understand a question, ask that it be explained;
- If a question calls for a "yes" or "no" answer, then your appropriate response should be "yes," "no," or perhaps "I don't recall," or "I don't know."
- Stick to the facts and testify to only that which you personally know, but don't be wishy-washy. Be positive and don't back down on your testimony as to those things about which you are reasonably certain.
- Testify only to "basic facts" and do not attempt to give opinions or estimates (e.g., of time and distance) unless you have good reasons for knowing such matters

- If you don’t know, admit it. Some witnesses think they should have an answer for every question asked. You most likely cannot know all the facts and you do yourself a disservice if you attempt to testify to facts with which you are not acquainted. It is imperative that you be honest and straightforward in your testimony.

Remember, perhaps the most important aspect of your case is you and the appearance you make to the Judge. If you give the appearance of earnestness, fairness, honesty, and of being certain about the facts to which you testify, and if in giving your testimony you keep in mind the suggestions herein made, you will be taking a great stride toward successful and satisfactory completion of the litigation in which you are involved.

Bear in mind if you hear me say “Objection to Form” - that means I think it’s a misleading or confusing question. You should strongly consider asking the questioner to re-phrase the question unless you're very confident you understand the question being asked of you.

How to Respond to the Cross-Examination Questions Asked[15]

A. Tell the truth.
B. Never lose your temper.
C. Don't be afraid of the lawyers.
D. Speak slowly and clearly.
E. If you don't understand the question, ask that it be explained.
F. Answer all questions directly, giving concise answers to the question, and then stop talking.
G. Never volunteer any information. Wait until the question is asked—answer it and stop. If you can answer "yes" or "no," do so and stop.
H. Stick to the facts and testify to only that which you personally know, but don't be wishy-washy. Be positive and don't back down on

---

[15] Adapted from "Family Law Depositions," 2d Ed., Nichols & Phillips, Juris Publishing (2022).

your testimony as to those things about which you are reasonably certain.

I. Testify only to "basic facts" and do not attempt to give opinions or estimates of time and distance unless you have a good reason for knowing such matters.

J. If you don't know, admit it. Some witnesses think they should have an answer for every question asked. You cannot know all the facts and you do yourself a disservice if you attempt to testify to facts with which you are not acquainted. It is imperative that you be honest and straightforward in your testimony.

K. Justice requires only that a witness tell his story to the best of his ability. Remember, perhaps the most important aspect of your lawsuit is you and the appearance you make. If you give the appearance of earnestness, fairness, honesty and of being certain about the facts to which you testify, and, if in giving your discovery deposition you keep in mind the suggestions herein made, you will be taking a great stride toward successful and satisfactory completion of the litigation in which you are involved.

Direct examination—Sample[16]

Q. Please state your name and address for the record.

A. Mary Smith. I live at 49 Elm Street, Albany, New York.

Q. Are you the plaintiff in this action for divorce?

A. Yes, I am.

Q. When and where were you married to the defendant?

A. We were married on August 5, 1982.

---

16 New York Matrimonial Law and Practice, Timothy Tippins, Thompson Reuters, § 18:29 (2022). This sample is only to illustrate the format of the questioning & will not bear relation to the actual questions which will be posed to you by the attorney.

Q. Are there any children of this marriage?

A. No.

Q. Is there any other action pending in any court to which you and the defendant are parties which seeks the same or similar relief as is sought in the present action?

A. No.

Q. Has there ever been granted any judgment, order, or decree of divorce, separation, or annulment with respect to this marriage?

A. No.

Q. Were you a resident of New York State at the time this action was commenced?

A. Yes, I was.

Q. And for how long had you continuously resided in this state immediately prior to the commencement of this action?

A. Twenty-seven years.

Q. Are you employed and, if so, in what capacity?

A. I am an attorney engaged in private practice as a sole practitioner.

Q. How long have you been an attorney?

A. Seven years.

Q. Did there come a time after your marriage when you and your husband separated?

A. Yes, there did.

Q. When was that?

A. August 5, 1982, the same day we were married.

Q. Would you please tell the court of the circumstances which surrounded that separation?

A. We had planned to move into the house where I was already living. I had purchased that house two years before our marriage. My husband wanted me to add his name to the deed. I didn't want to do so at that time and when I said so he became very upset and he called me several foul names.

Q. When did this conversation take place?

A. On our wedding night.

Q. Where did it occur?

A. In the bridal suite at the Waldorf.

Q. What reason, if any, did you have for not placing his name on the deed?

A. I wanted to make sure that our marriage was solid before I did that. Also, the house was fully paid for and he hadn't made any contribution toward the house, so I really didn't see any reason why I should do so.

Q. You testified that he called you certain names. Would you please tell the court specifically what he called you?

A. He called me a "greedy whore" and a "worthless slut."

Q. What, if anything, else occurred on your wedding night?

A. Well, he continued to insist that I should put his name on the deed and he got so mad that he finally hit me in the face with a handful of ice cubes and then he stormed out of the room.

Q. When did you next see him?

A. Six months later.

Q. Would you tell the court what the circumstances were when you next saw him?

A. He showed up on my doorstep with his suitcase and said he wanted to make the marriage work.

Q. What, if anything, did you tell him?

A. I told him to get lost.

Q. What, if anything, did he do?

A. He punched me in the mouth.

Q. What did you do?

A. I slammed the door and called the police. Then I went to the hospital and had stitches in my mouth where he hit me.

Q. When did you next see your husband?

A. Not until today when I arrived at the courthouse.

Q. Was there any property of any kind acquired by you between August 5, 1982, the date of your marriage, and March 3, 1983, the date this action was commenced?

A. No.

Q. Did you work in your profession during that time?

A. No.

Q. Why didn't you work?

A. I was simply too upset by what my husband had done to me, walking out like that and everything.

Q. Other than not being able to work, what effect, if any did your husband's conduct have on you?

A. I couldn't eat properly. I lost twenty-one pounds. I cried myself to sleep every night. I almost had a nervous breakdown.

Q. Have you since returned to work?

A. Yes.

Q. When did you do so?

A. In April of 1983.

Q. Are you presently self-supporting?

A. I am.

Q. Thank you. No further questions.

About The Author

David Bliven graduated with honors from Syracuse University in 1993 with a B.A. in Sociology. He went on to serve as a statistician with the NYS Commission on City Court Judicial Reallocation with the Office of the Deputy Chief Administrative Judge. He then attended New York Law School where he graduated in 1997 with honors and ranked within the top 15% of his class.

Shortly after graduating, he served as a prosecutor for nearly 3 years with the NYC Administration for Children's Services. While at ACS he prosecuted child support, child abuse & neglect and foster care cases on behalf of the City of New York.

After leaving the prosecutor position, Mr. Bliven opened his present practice in 2000. His practice is currently devoted 100% to Divorce & Family Court cases.

Mr. Bliven has an "AV" rating from Martindale-Hubbell (the highest possible rating in both Legal Ability & Ethical Standards), a perfect 10.0 rating from Avvo ("Superb" rating) and is listed in the "Super Lawyers" directory by Thompson Reuters (a distinction given to less than 5% of all attorneys in each field of practice). He is also a "Certified Financial Litigator" and was honored as a "Super Lawyer" for the NY Metro & Westchester area by *Westchester Magazine* in their October, 2019 issue.

Mr. Bliven has authored the books "Navigating Your New York Divorce Case, "Navigating Your New York Family Court Case" and "Navigating Your New York High Net Worth Divorce Case." His articles have been published in the New York Law Journal, Nolo.com and Westchester Lawyer Magazine.

TESTIMONIALS

- Anonymous: "During a time, when it seemed as my life was about to fall apart, Mr. Bliven was there to make sure I was protected. Mr. Bliven was there to make sure every "T" was crossed and every "I" was dotted. He made sure I was entitled to my fair share. When children are involved in a divorce, I wanted to make sure they were taken care of for the foreseeable future. Mr. Bliven made it his duty to fight for me when he felt I deserved more retribution. He fought tooth and nail for the needs of my children as well as for me. During a time when things looked bleak, Mr. Bliven made sure my legal and financial needs are taken care of. When beginning this venture, I was scared that I would walk off of this with only my "shirt", but Mr. Bliven made it his job to make sure I was able to resume my life without looking back. I want to thank Mr. Bliven and I would recommend him to anyone who is and is thinking about filing for a divorce."

- Jonathan: "Mr. Bliven came very highly recommended to me by a friend who used to practice family law and had transitioned into other areas of legal practice. I was not disappointed. Mr. Bliven was thoroughly knowledgeable and highly attentive as he helped me smoothly resolve complex child support matters involving international issues of competing jurisdictions. Having had a number of attorneys in the course of my divorce and child custody/support matters over the last 18 years, I believe I am experienced to know that Mr. Bliven is a top family law expert."

- Lou: "Mr. Bliven represented me in a child support case. I was very pleased with the services provided by Mr. Bliven. He is professional, courteous, and knows his stuff! I am completely gratified with the outcome of my case. Thanks to Mr. Bliven's knowledge of family law. Mr. Bliven kept me up to date on all matters pertaining to my case and his billing is fair and accurate for the work he puts into the case. I would certainly recommend him to anyone that is seeking a topnotch lawyer in the area family court."

- Teri Colon: "Although I have not met with Mr. Bliven yet. I contacted his office on a Friday of a Holiday Weekend. His office's response was immediate and I was treated with respect as if I was already a client. His staff took the time to email me immediately and when I called I was given an appointment that accommodates my schedule. Custody matters are very sensitive and clients can be emotional. It was a relief to speak with someone who was not only professional and courtesy, but also showed genuine concern. I look forward to my consultation with Mr. Bliven."

- Ariane: "Mr. Bliven was knowledgeable, informative, and an incredible strategist. He used all of my legal rights to defend me in my case and was extremely professional to work with. I can't thank him enough for his ability to use our rights as law-abiding citizens and to get the job done. David consulted with me on all motions before revealing them to the court or to any other parties. For this I thank him and am grateful for his diligence in representation."

- Gregg: "Although I subscribe to a legal plan through my union (I'm a teacher), I decided to retain Mr. Bliven based on our initial consultation. He seemed much better versed than the less expensive "plan" attorney I spoke to in the child support matter I brought to him. Mr. Bliven scanned the paperwork I brought with me to the consultation and immediately developed a strategy using various points of law. Mr. Bliven kept in constant contact with me and "cc'd" me on all correspondence he and my ex-wife's attorney had via email or hard-copy. Mr. Bliven's courtroom demeanor was just as I had hoped it would be; vocal and on point. Ultimately, my ex-wife and I reached a fair compromise that did not follow the default percentages NY State dictates. I would definitely retain again should the need arise."

- A Satisfied Client: "Navigating family court for personal reasons can be quite intimidating, even for folks who have interfaced with court officers and judges for professional purposes. That said, Bliven was nothing short of extremely knowledgeable, courteous and very attuned with the emotional experience that comes with the process. I highly recommend Bliven if you are seeking consultation and representation with a child support and/or custody case!"

****

More Testimonials may be found on David Bliven's website (http://www.blivenlaw.net/Testimonials.shtml) and at Avvo (https://www.avvo.com/attorneys/10463-ny-david-bliven-952796.html#client_reviews).

*   *   *   *

If you appreciated the information given to you in this book, Mr. Bliven would appreciate a review of the book on Amazon and/or a Google review:

https://g.page/law-offices-of-david-bliven-933/review?rc

INDEX

S

T

U

Notes

Made in the USA
Las Vegas, NV
03 November 2026

57425297R00095